Word Bird™ Bird

Makes Words
With Hen

Published in the United States of America by The Child's World®, Inc.
PO Box 326
Chanhassen, MN 55317-0326
800-599-READ
www.childsworld.com

Project Manager Mary Berendes
Editor Katherine Stevenson, Ph.D.
Designer Ian Butterworth

Library of Congress Cataloging-in-Publication Data
Moncure, Jane Belk.
Word Bird makes words with Hen : a short "e" adventure / by Jane Belk Moncure.
p. cm.
Summary: When his father brings him some new word puzzles,
Word Bird makes up more words with his friend Hen, and each word that
they make up leads them into a new activity.
ISBN 1-56766-902-6 (lib. bdg.)
[1. Vocabulary. 2. Birds—Fiction. 3. Chickens—Fiction.] I. Title.
PZ7.M739 Wnh 2001
[E]—dc21
00-010893

Word Bird™

Makes Words With Hen

by Jane Belk Moncure

illustrated by Chris McEwan

One day, Papa came home with some new word puzzles.

WORD
PUZZLES
Short e

"Do you like word puzzles?" asked Papa.

"You bet," said Word Bird.

Word Bird put

t with en.

What did Word Bird make?

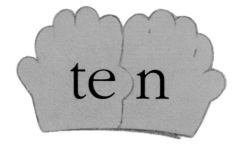

te n

1 2 3 4 5 6 7 8 9 10

Word Bird counted to ten and back again. Can you?

Then Word Bird put

p with en.

What did Word Bird make?

p en

"I can write words with
a pen," Word Bird said.
"I can write ten."

And Word Bird did.

Then Word Bird put

h with en.

What did Word Bird make?

h en

Just then, Hen came over
to play.

"Hi, Hen."

"I can put word puzzles together," said Hen. She put

e with gg.

What word did Hen make?

"Let's make an
Easter-egg tree,"
said Word Bird.

It was a nice egg tree.
But they made a mess!

Mama said, "Please clean up this mess."
So they did.

Then Word Bird put

j with et.

What did Word Bird make?

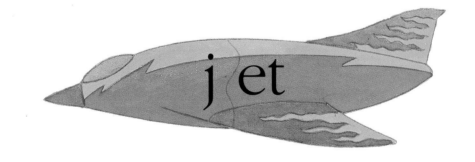

j et

"Let's go for a jet ride,"
said Word Bird.

So they did.

Then Hen put

ch with est.

What word did Hen make?

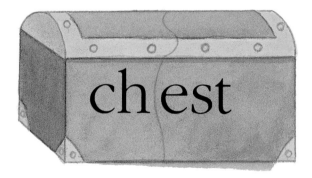

chest

"Let's see what is in this chest," said Word Bird.

The chest was full of shells—seashells.

"Let's play with the shells," said Word Bird.

They made a mess!
What did Mama say?

Word Bird said, "I will
make another word."
Word Bird put

t with ent.

What did Word Bird make?

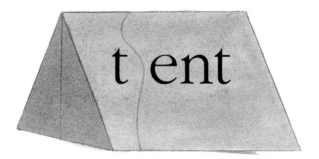

t ent

"I have a tent,"
said Word Bird.

"Let's play in your tent,"
said Hen. So they did.

They played in the tent
until ten o'clock.

Later, it began to snow.

"I will make another
word," said Word Bird.

Word Bird put

sl with ed.

What did Word Bird make?

sl ed

"I have a sled,"
said Word Bird.

"Let's get on the sled,"
Hen said.

They went down the hill
on the sled ten times.

Then Mama called,
"Come in, Word Bird."

Mama said,
"Look at your face!"

Word Bird looked in
the mirror. Word Bird
saw RED!

You can read more word
puzzles with Word Bird.

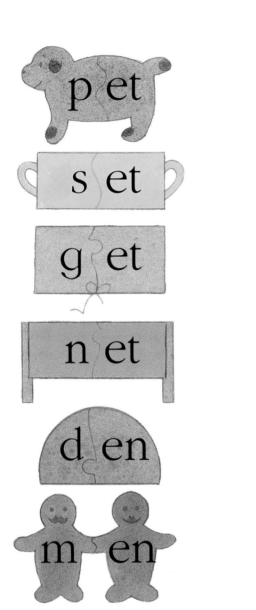

p et

s et

g et

n et

d en

m en

b ell

s ell

f ell

t ell

p ep

st ep

Now you can make some word puzzles.